Love Letters to My Body

OTHER BOOKS BY NICOLE C. AYERS

Love Notes to My Body

Writing My Way to (Self-)Love:
A Guided Journal to Help You
Love Your Body, One Part at a Time

Love Letters to My Body

Writing My Way to (Self-)Love

Nicole C. Ayers

Illustrated by
Mica Gadhia

SPARK Publications
Charlotte, North Carolina

Love Letters to My Body
Writing My Way to (Self-)Love

©2019 by Nicole C. Ayers. All rights reserved. No part of this book may be used or reproduced in any manner whatsoever without written permission from the author, except in the case of brief quotations in critical articles and reviews. For permissions requests, please contact the author at nicole@nicolecayers.com.

Illustrations by Mica Gadhia

Book designed, produced, and published
by SPARK Publications, SPARKpublications.com
Charlotte, North Carolina

Printed in the United States of America.
Softcover, February 2020, ISBN: 978-1-943070-77-0
E-book, February 2020, ISBN: 978-1-943070-78-7
Library of Congress Control Number: 2020900904

Dedication

To Campbell Faye and Jude Rae, my daughters
May you never question how worthy you are.
I love you.

Dear Readers,

I'm many things: a woman and a writer and an editor and a wife and a mother, to name a few. You'll read about my funny and supportive husband, Terry, and my brilliant and brave daughters, Campbell and Jude, in these pages. These are my people, and they've taught me so many lessons.

Photo courtesy of Corrie Fewell, BlueSky Photo Artists

I'm sharing my personal love letters to my body with the wish that my struggles with my body will shine a light on your own. Our stories and experiences are different, but I bet you'll catch glimpses of yourself here. My hope is that reading these letters will make you curious about your own relationship with your body. If after reading and reflecting on your own body parts, you're a smidge closer to accepting your body just as it is, know that I'm cheering so loudly for you. And if you're not ready to consider a relationship with your body, I'm celebrating you too. This work is a lifelong process that will be waiting whenever you're ready.

Why love letters? Because I spent the majority of my life hating my body, or at least parts of it. If I wasn't actively hating it, I was often trying to improve it. Or dissing it. Or thinking—sometimes even saying—hateful words about it.

I realized that I couldn't love myself in a real, true way until I made peace with my body and accepted all of it. That sounds so positive and compassionate, except I had no idea how to go about falling in love with a body that I didn't want to live in, much less learn to love.

So I made it my mission to figure out what actionable steps I could take to learn to love all of my body. I started by looking in the mirror and saying, "I love you." Hokey, but helpful. I practiced affirmations and wrote positive notes on my mirror. And then I started writing love notes to different body parts in my journal.

This became a powerful practice because it's awfully hard to write a love note to somebody you hate. Some of my notes were silly, many were poignant, and others showed me I had anger and sadness and pain and distrust roiling just under the surface. If I was going to love all the parts of my body, then I was going to have to dive into those feelings. It's a long, hard journey to dismantle decades of ingrained lessons about what equals beauty and worth in our society, and I had a lot of beliefs to unpack and examine. But I was finally ready to reclaim my body—from my family of origin, from my children, from the media, from everything and every person who'd made me believe that it had to look or be a certain way.

These love letters have healed festering wounds I've carried around for decades. They've helped me release the suffering I lived with around certain body parts and their experiences. Most of all, they've helped me accept myself fully, and dare I say it? I've learned to love all of myself, every part.

I'd be lying if I didn't admit to still cringing sometimes when I see a photo of myself. But this is a journey I'll stay on until the very end, until every wound has been healed, because my body is worth the boundless love I have for it. I am worth it.

And so are you.

Imagine as you read my love letters that I'm walking the wild, overgrown path before us with a machete, chopping down all the roots and vines that are trying to strangle us. My precious daughters are right behind me. We're waiting on you to join our conga line as we dance our way through the fire and into the wilderness of acceptance and vulnerability and love.

Love, Nicole

One Last Note

These letters are about *my* body. You are welcome here, without judgment, however you and your body show up: fat, skinny, toned, flabby, curvy, big-bosomed, flat-chested, tall, short . . .

And these letters describe *my* experiences. You are welcome here, without judgment, whether you shave, pluck, and thread every stray hair or whether you've thrown out all the hair-removal tools; whether you monitor your calories or eat everything you want; whether you move your body as part of a weight-loss plan or because movement brings you pleasure.

You are welcome here, without judgment.

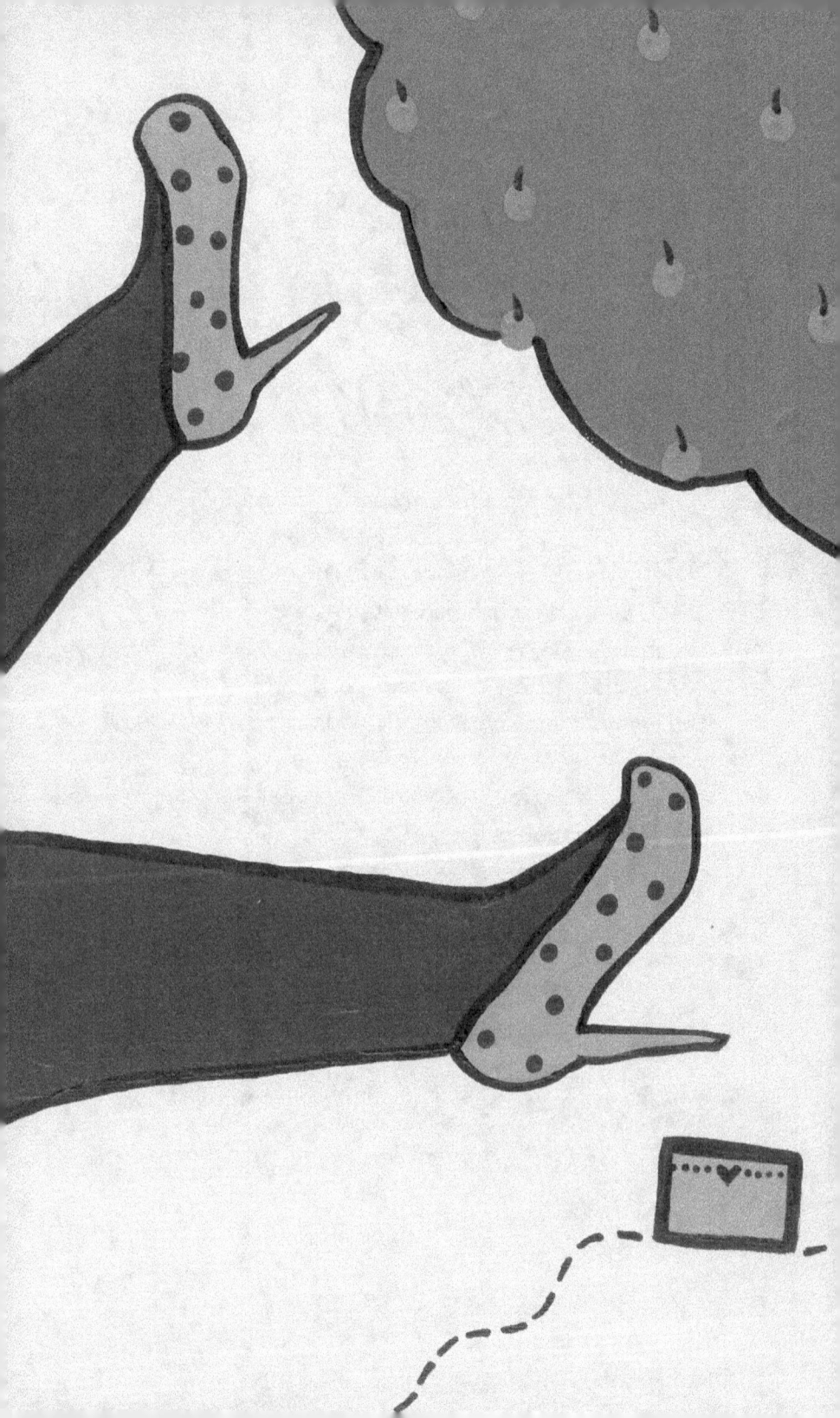

Table of Contents

    The particular order of these essays unfolded in a gloriously illogical mess that probably only makes sense to me because that's how my healing tends to happen. Things show up when they're ready, and there's no straight path to follow.

    If you like order, try not to get too caught up wondering why I didn't take a logical head-to-feet approach. You can read the essays in any order you choose.

    Some of you won't even notice the order. You, too, can read the essays in any order you choose.

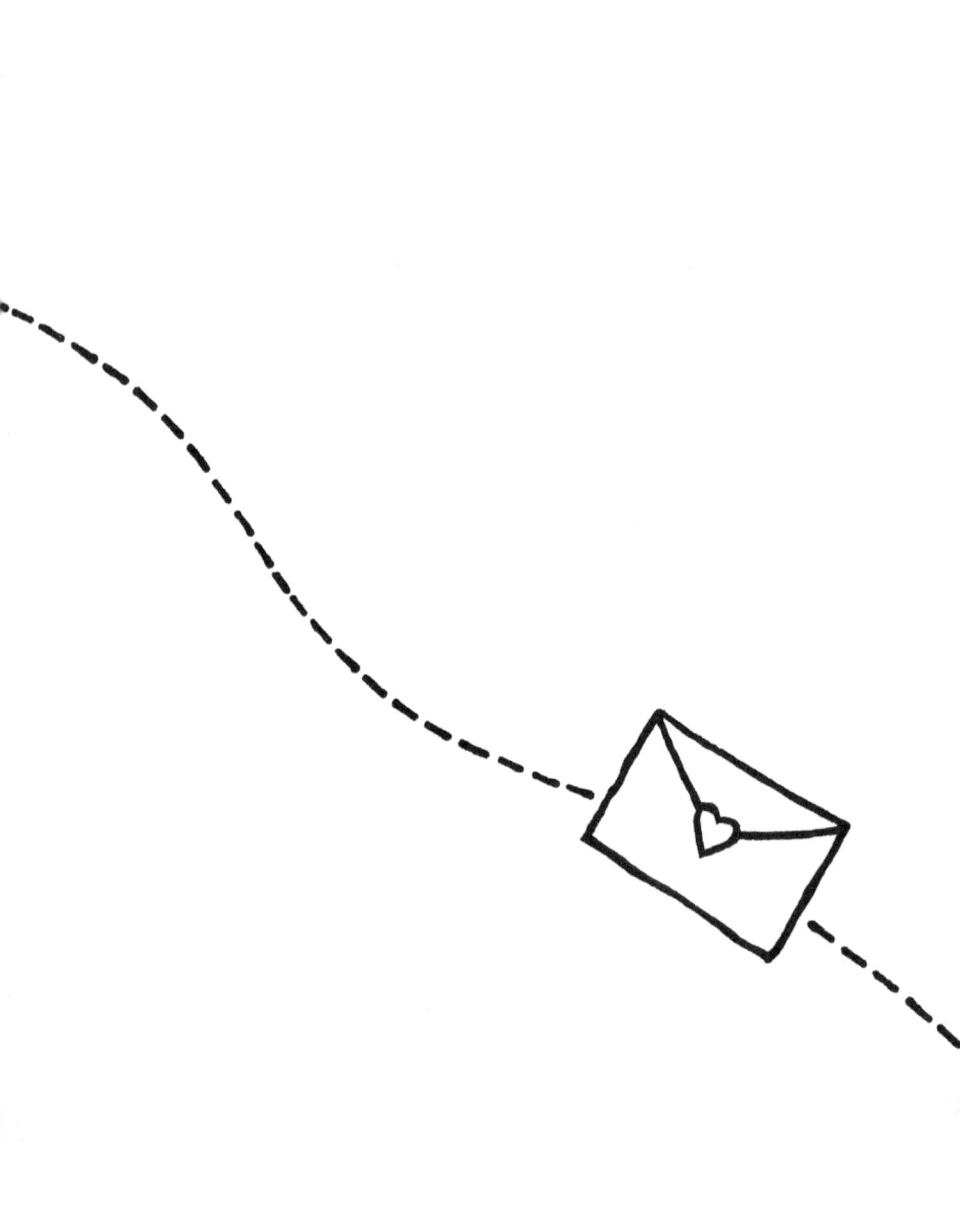

Dear...

Voice 1

Hair 7

Front Tooth 15

Eyebrows 21

Taste Buds 25

Ring Finger 31

Birthmark 39

Knees 45

Back 51

Boobs 55

Tear Factory 61

Hands 67

Belly 71

Parts I Haven't Written To (Yet) 75

Dear Voice,

You're such a complex creation. So many body parts in my vocal tract (my larynx, vocal cords, tongue, and teeth, to name a few) must all work together to generate your unique sound. When I think about how special you are, I realize I owe you an apology for all the times I shushed you without thought to your feelings, stuffing you down as if you didn't matter.

Silencing you meant I could tag along with my mom and her friends. Or I could pretend to read and eavesdrop on their conversations. I was so ravenous for information. What was going on? What were they talking about? What were their plans? Could I be included, or would I be dropped off at my grandmother's?

Swallowing my feelings and silencing you meant my mom would love me. I'd seen her eviscerate the store clerk who didn't provide the customer service she was expecting. She'd cut loved ones off when they crossed her. No more relationship. As terrible as her temper was, when she loved someone, it was like being loved by the sun. She was charismatic and kind and fun. I didn't want to lose that just because there was something to say.

I never talked back as a kid. I would see my friends being brutal to their mothers, and I would marvel at their mothers' calm responses. I didn't feel safe enough in my mother's love to be sassy. I knew she wouldn't tolerate it, which meant she wouldn't tolerate me. I used to cry when she braided my hair because I was tenderheaded in addition to being tenderhearted, and she'd fuss as if I was wrong for speaking up that I felt pain.

    My intuition was proved right. I knew that giving you free rein would result in abandonment. At fifteen, when my mom's live-in boyfriend made living with her feel unsafe, I left my mother's home and moved in with my dad. Things were so tense between my mom and me, and we had a fight on the phone. It's the first time I remember us fighting. I let you scream a curse at her and hung up. My mom and I didn't speak for two years. Even after we reconnected, I wasn't allowed to use you to apologize or ask for an apology. We steered clear of conversations that could lead to disagreements. I believed that if I let you out and shared less-agreeable opinions, she'd leave again. I'm not sure what fears drove her to silence, but I assume they were similar to my own.

    Silencing you also meant my dad would want to hang out. When I was very small and quite the chatterbox, he would take me fishing. He told me that talking would scare the fish away, so it was keep you quiet or don't go fishing. I started bringing books with me when I was a little bit older, which he interpreted as me not being interested in fishing. Maybe I wasn't. But books were an escape for me, a safety net of protection, a fort against conversation.

    He didn't talk about feelings, either. I didn't know how he felt about much of anything. Was he sad? Or mad? Or lonely? Was he trying to protect me or protect himself from all the feelings? And sometimes that stoicism looked mighty attractive. If I could hold you back, keep from emoting too much, then I wouldn't have to look at what hurt. If you couldn't name it, then I didn't have to claim it.

    I couldn't silence you completely, though. You poured out in thoughts and feelings and desires and wonders and fears in journals. You kept me sane while I was trying to navigate my grief and teenage angst. I detailed the risky ways I was trying to fill the holes bleeding me dry. And then, in a betrayal that cut so deep, when my stepmom convinced my dad to read my journal, I realized you weren't safe in the written world either. I didn't let you out in writing again for more than a decade, even after my dad bought me a diary with a lock and key as an apology.

    As a younger adult, I was still so afraid of how I'd be perceived if I shared all the things I thought and believed. I'd share bits of myself with my boyfriend and my book club and my best friend and my family and my coworkers and my roommates, but rarely did any one person hear everything. The only time I was comfortable letting you out fully was on the stage or while reading aloud to students. Pretending to be a character who was angry or scared or lonely or sad or anguished or jealous or mean or ashamed was a release valve for you, a way I could let you shout or whisper or sing without being displeasing to anyone in real life.

    But now I believe in you, in your power. I found unconditional love in a partner who is so comfortable in his own skin. Terry modeled what it looks like to speak up and say what you want to say until I let you practice those moves, too. Once, when Terry and I were going through a difficult time, the only way I knew how to tell him how I felt was to write him a letter. The letter didn't bridge the divide between us. Your clumsy attempt at unfiltered honesty had made it wider. I'd vomited on the page and then shared the mess without sitting with it first to make sure that was really how I felt. I remember being so scared. If my most trusted person couldn't handle you, then who could? Turns out, he could, but it took hard work on both our parts.

Figuring out that he couldn't read my mind, even in letter form, that I had to let you share what was going on in my head and my heart, deepened our relationship and gave me courage to let you loose on the rest of the world. Now I model what it looks like to let you be honest about what you need so my daughters know how to use their voices to stay visible. I tell them that I will never leave them for speaking their truths.

I think you're smart and insightful and kind. I love the way you translate across the page. I'm quite gobsmacked sometimes when I read my own writing because it sounds exactly like you. You have some special magic to make that happen.

You are powerful.

I'm learning how vulnerable I feel when I use you with different audiences and in more public arenas. But also how strong I am. Thank you for showing me that I can be both vulnerable and strong at the same time. Sometimes I'm still afraid to speak up and out, whether for myself or for others, but I don't let fear hold me back anymore. I know the people who matter most to me won't abandon me. And I won't abandon you ever again.

I was born to unleash you.

Love, Me

Dear Hair,

You have always been a signpost for where I am and what I value. For the first half of my life—so until I was in my early twenties—you were long, long, long, straight, and brown. I remember being told how pretty you were and how long hair is the epitome of beauty (also, that men like long hair) and that no one wanted me to cut you. I practiced being pretty. I wanted the people I loved to think I was beautiful, so I was happy to conform to their expectations and keep you long. I didn't ask you what you wanted. I just accepted everyone else's opinion without questioning.

When I was a toddler, I'd beg my grandmother to roll your wispy strands on hot rollers so that I could be just like her. She was one of the most beautiful women in my world, and I wanted her to shower me with the same attention she gave to her hair, which she lovingly did. Already, I was internalizing the notion that styling you just so equaled beauty and love.

In the second grade, I had to wear you in a tight French braid every day after I got lice. You were as tender as my sensitive soul, and it hurt when my mom pulled you so tight. My tear factory often cranked up. You've picked up lice four times since then. That's an excessive amount of lice, I agree. Lice don't care much about your defenses. They think you are lovely.

Nicole C. Ayers

In middle school, I teased the crap out of your bangs and shellacked them with Aqua Net, so I could look like everybody else, even though I always thought that you looked like teased poop rolls on top of my head. To change things up, I got a spiral perm so you could rock fake curls and huge bangs. It took hours to get you styled just so, and the hairspray would build up and flake, making it look like you had dandruff. Still, I persevered. I didn't even stop to think about the things I might be sacrificing—time and creativity and originality—to fit in. Being included was important to me. I liked to be liked.

Not feeling like I fit in with my family of origin taught me how to be a chameleon. Terry used to call me Tim Wakefield, the baseball pitcher who could pitch in every rotation, because I was always able to move in so many different circles. I didn't have a "group" of my own, but I skirted the edges of everyone else's. I could bend myself just enough to blend in and get along with everyone. I could be the family girl, the academic girl, the theater girl, the teacher girl, the party girl, the religious girl, the helpful girl. Keeping you long and sleek and smooth made it easy for me to slide in and out of social interactions. The easy entrée you provided me was the trade I made for putting up with your weight and your heat.

And then at seventeen, when I was at the Fine Arts Center (FAC) for theater, I desperately wanted to dye you purple. The kids at FAC were the out-of-the-box kids who dyed their hair and pierced their faces and kissed girls (if they were girls) and boys (if they were boys) just to see how other people would react. And while I wanted purple hair, I also wanted to continue being a chameleon. I wouldn't fit in very well in my other groups (think honors classes back at my home school and the countrified potheads my boyfriend hung out with) if you were purple.

My dad said, "No way." And while I didn't always take my dad's rules seriously, by that time, I'd made peace with them. I'd already gotten most of the wildness out of my system and was healing the wounds that had created the wildness. And I still felt guilty for the grief I'd caused when he read my diary, so I didn't push the dye job. In the same way he didn't want to talk about feelings and being vulnerable, he didn't want me to be vulnerable either, open to being hurt by others. I think he viewed purple hair as something silly, something that would put me in danger of living outside the norms, something that would make me more foreign (to him) and open to ridicule. I understood that he wanted to protect me, even if I found his protection as stifling as wearing you down on a hot day.

Plus, I was terrified that I'd somehow ruin you and have to cut you off. Remember, you were pretty when you were long, and everybody liked me that way.

What would you have done if I wasn't so worried about fitting in and being liked? Would you have wanted to be so short and have me shave my head, like Sinead O'Connor? Remember how cool I thought she looked and how many times I played "Nothing Compares to You"? Or would you have wanted an outlandish punk Mohawk? I know you would have been purple, no doubt. Probably pink, too.

A few years later, I'd finally had enough of hair for everybody else. It was just me and you and what we wanted—finally. I broke up with my longtime boyfriend, and I was getting ready to start my final year of college. I was ready to go places. So we got our first pixie cut.

The stylist was terrified because you were seriously long when I walked in, and I gave her a picture and said, "Do this, please." She kept asking if I wanted an in-between cut to work my way up to the pixie, but I refused. I had my gumption up, and we weren't going home without lightening your load. She turned my chair away from the mirror and cut so much of you away. And I loved you!

I felt so sassy and independent. I was making choices for myself. I was liberated from the tyranny of your length and all the expectations of other people that I associated with it. I realized my neck was gorgeous. I'd found so much more time in my day now that I didn't have to spend an hour on you. You didn't make me feel hot and itchy at night because you weren't wrapping yourself around my face when I slept. I was in less danger of being snatched by the ponytail in a parking lot. And you weren't going to catch pesky lice from anybody anymore.

My family and friends had mixed reactions. My grandmother cried when she saw me. That stung. My uncle made jokes about my sexuality. That stung too. And pissed me off. Name-calling sucks. But mostly, people thought I was cute. Maybe not pretty anymore, but definitely cute. And still pleasing.

That first dramatic haircut helped me test the waters of nonconformity. Look, I get it. Lots of women have short hair. But cute white heterosexual Southern girls did not, and I had lived in that box of labels (and privileges) my whole life. It was scary to show up and let the back of my neck (a little piece of myself) be seen. What I figured out was that the only person I had to please with you was myself, though. So I began to play.

You've been all different lengths since then. You've been really dark and almost blonde. Once, you had an awesome dye job that flipped; when I parted you to the right, you were dark, and when I parted you to the left, you had chunky blonde streaks. But you were never purple. Until now.

Since *The Hunger Games* movie came out (maybe before then), rainbow-colored hair has become mainstream. I see lots of folks out and about in the world with colored tresses, and I have a few friends who take risks with their hair, but most of the people I see on a day-to-day basis do not. You're a novelty at neighborhood gatherings and PTO meetings and the dentist's office. But I don't care what anybody else in this world thinks about you anymore because I think you're awesome. Not once has my mother, grandmother, or mother-in-law commented on my hair since I started dyeing it funky colors. My dad did ask me why I'd dyed you blue and just said, "Huh," when I told him I'd dyed you because I wanted to.

I know I've grown into my own skin because I don't care if they like it or not. And I appreciate that they are choosing to be quiet if they can't be kind. There was a time not so long ago that their silence would have hurt my feelings, but the part of me that has always needed to be pleasing and liked has finally begun to see the light. If I like it, then that is enough.

You are bright with color, which is a billboard for the boldness I feel in showing up as myself. Turning forty felt like an unfettering. I'd heard friends say how wonderful turning forty was for them. It was the same for me. I'm not sure what the magical elixir was. Maybe beginning our fifth decade meant I'd acquired some wisdom. Maybe it's because I was almost a brand-new person again, someone who didn't care about most people's opinions anymore. They say our cells regenerate every seven years, meaning we're a whole new creation. Maybe I began to love you more. If forty means I'm about halfway through this life of mine, then I don't want to waste a minute more on the nonsense of making choices based on others' opinions.

A little thrill of joy runs through me every time I glimpse a streak of purple or pink or blue in your brown strands. I love the juxtaposition of the bright colors with the peekaboo oil slick. Why did it take me so long to dip you in the rainbow? I'll never deny myself the joy of playing with you again. I definitely plan to be one of those blue-haired old ladies.

All the manipulative locks I'd bound myself with, hoping for the approval of others, have fallen away. I know you're beautiful. I know I'm beautiful, too. Not because someone else said so, but because I'm being exactly who I was meant to be.

Love, Me

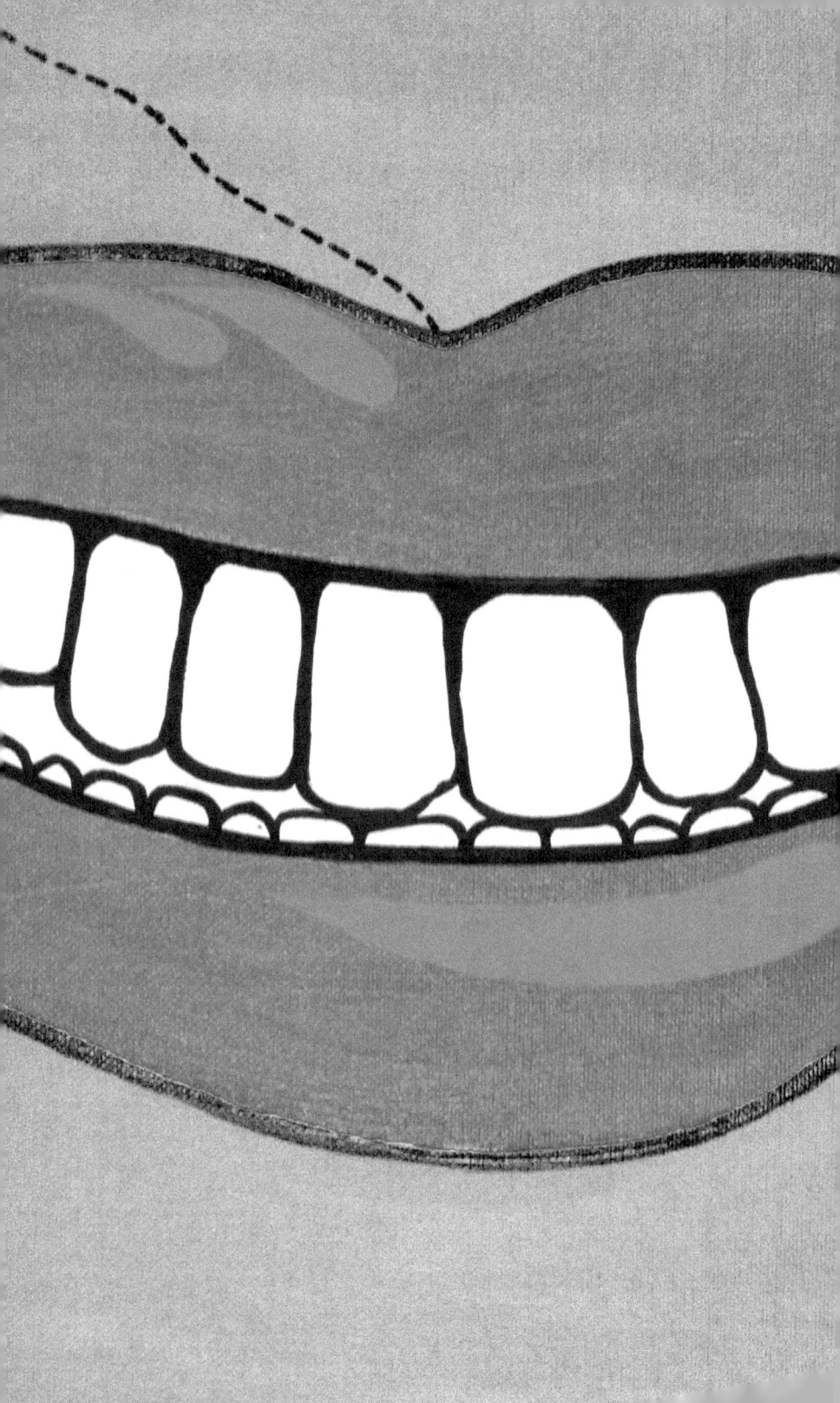

Dear Front Tooth,

Do you remember that afternoon? Mom and Dad had just separated, and we were all trying to adjust to this new way of seeing each other. Daddy worked swing shifts, so he'd spend time with us on random days.

It was warm and sunny. It must have been summer, because they separated the first night of our annual beach vacation, and school hadn't started yet. Daddy had picked me up and taken me to my elementary school so we could play on the playground. It's the only time I remember being on a playground with either of my parents. I don't know if that means they didn't take me to playgrounds very often or if I was too young to hold onto those everyday sorts of memories, the minutia of a young girl's world.

The playground was deserted, and no teacher would tell me to be careful. I loved that delicious feeling of being somewhere I maybe wasn't supposed to be. (Can you go to school when school's not in session?) I'd run as fast as I could, then shriek when Daddy was close enough to catch me. I'd veer away and laugh wildly.

I was laughing and giggling and clambering all over the playground equipment, being daring as I climbed higher than teachers let me.

I was pulling myself up the outside of the slide to get away quick. The metal bars were warm and slippery under my sweaty hands. I planned to throw my leg over the protective bar, heave myself onto the platform, then slide down and away. Giggling, screaming, climbing—*BAM!*

I cracked you smack into one of those bars.

Oh, poor tooth! There were blood and tears and rough edges where a bit of you had gone missing. Playdate with Daddy over.

I have a lot of sympathy for the little girl I was, who just wanted to spend time with her dad. I remember feeling like it was my fault rather than an accident—one of many times when I bought the lie that I wasn't strong enough or smart enough or athletic enough to push my body to new limits. If I hadn't broken you, Front Tooth, then we could have kept having fun. And my mom wouldn't have yelled at my dad when he brought me home. And maybe if I had been better, they'd love each other enough that I wouldn't have to have those weird playground dates when my dad was off work.

I don't remember if someone told me you were jacked up, or if I just accepted that you were because you were no longer perfect. The women in my family have been plagued for generations by perfection's sweet deceptions. If they can be perfect, then they will be safe. I accepted the lessons of perfection without question. I wanted to be safe, too.

My mom suffered a terrible fall as a teenager and broke her front teeth. After lots of dental work, her teeth gleamed when she smiled. Here we were with our own brokenness. You were the one missing a piece, but my parents' divorce left me with phantom gaps. I wanted to fix you so you'd be gleaming, too. If you were gleaming, you couldn't be broken. I wouldn't be broken, at least on the outside.

When I was a little older and my front teeth had stopped growing, my dentist suggested I could cover up your calcium-deposit spots, make you whiter, with a special bonding material.

"Can you cover up that chip, too?" I asked. I was thrilled when he said yes.

The bonding material ended up being much uglier than your little chip. The dentist handed me a mirror, and I was so disappointed. The white spots on my enamel and your chipped imperfection had been plastered over. Suddenly, you were thicker than you had been and felt strange when I ran my tongue across you. You weren't the gleaming white I'd envisioned either.

I'll never forget being at lunch in middle school and a huge piece of the bonding just flaking off. I was mortified. At first, I thought I'd lost you completely. I felt panicked and relieved at the same time. Relieved, of course, because you were still there, but panicked because I had no idea how to get the bonding back on. My friends were curious and confused about why I was so upset. I didn't know how to explain what had happened because I didn't want them to know I had fake stuff on my teeth. How shameful! Part of looking perfect meant no one would know when I was faking it.

I had to wait several days to get the bonding redone at the dentist's office. I wouldn't smile or talk in case someone might see you. That process repeated itself several times over the years. My sham to make you perfect kept revealing me as a charlatan. It's tiresome to cover up the truth. Finally, I decided to remove the bonding.

It was such a relief to have that material buffed off and

just let your natural beauty—my natural beauty—shine through. I remember thinking that your chip was so huge, like half of you had been hacked off. Turns out, after the big reveal, you sported a small little divot that gave my smile some character. No one ever in my adult life has asked how you got that chip; that's how unnoticeable it is.

When I see your little chip now, with its edges smoothed by time, I remember that feeling of joy and wonder as I was climbing, not the pain of the accident or its emotional aftermath. Because that's where I choose to concentrate my attention. Because I've accepted that accidents happen, and that day I had an accident. Because I love you just exactly like you are, especially your tiny chip. What a perfect example that my imperfections are always more beautiful than hiding behind a veneer.

Love, Me

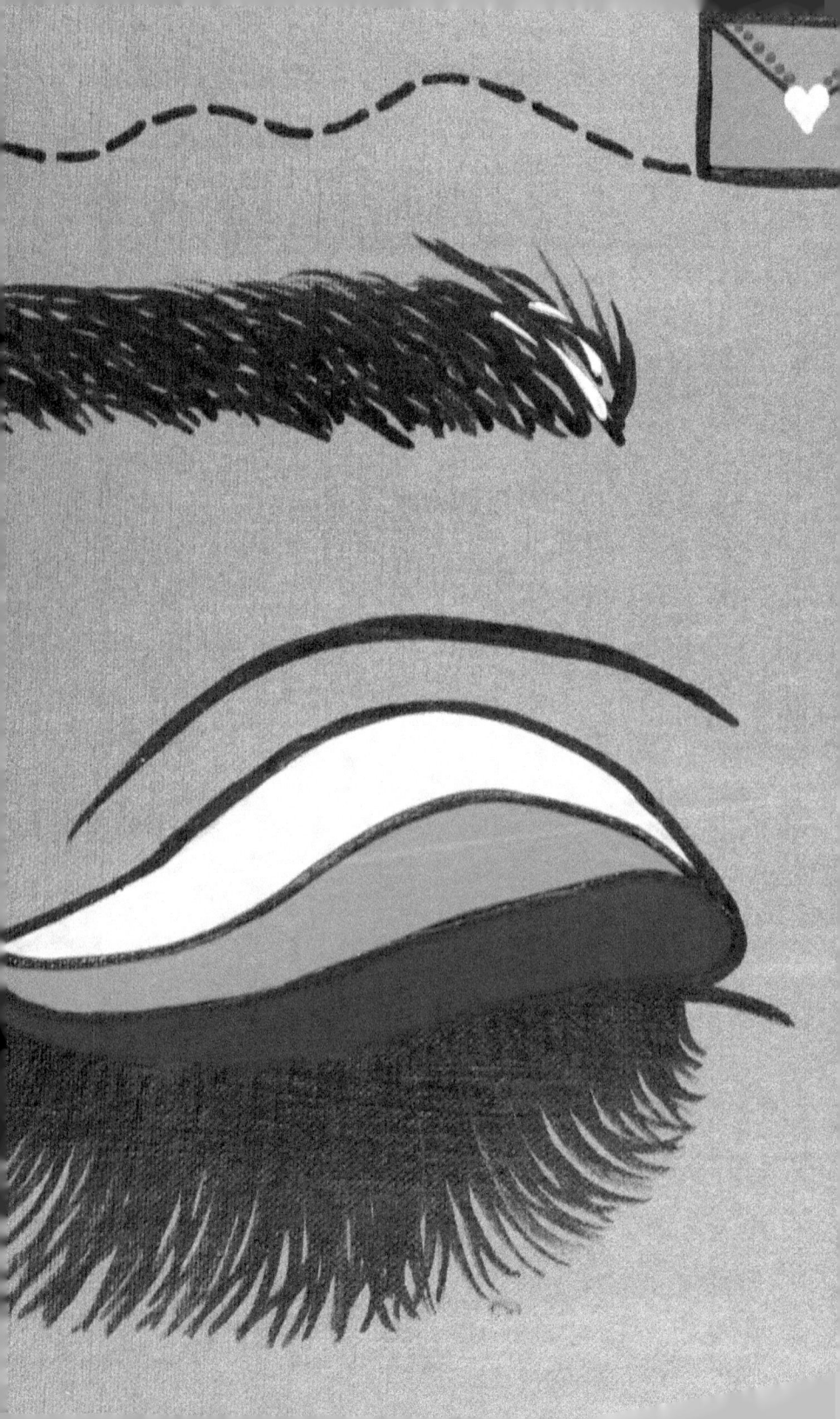

Dear Eyebrows,

You remind me so much of my dad. Every time I look closely at you, I see your dark thickness framing my eyes and realize that you are the exact same shape as my dad's. You are wild and unruly. And your hairs closest to my nose grow straight up. It makes me laugh because I imagine you saying, "You can't make me lie down. How dare you tell me what to do. I'll stand up if I want to."

I remember my mom always plucking her eyebrows with tweezers, snatching strays away. And the magazines I read featured articles discussing the best brow for my face's shape. I used a clear mascara-like gel in middle school that was meant to make you look just so. I think it was my dad's second wife who convinced me to wage war against you. To wage an unwinnable war against you. Unwinnable because you will never stop growing in riotous ways.

Nonetheless, I spent years torturing you, my poor eyebrows. First, I tried the tweezer-plucking method. It hurt, and I always thought there were so many of you to pluck that I'd get overwhelmed and quit.

Next, I tried hot wax. It was so seductive. The warm wax felt luscious, the pressing of the cotton strip over the wax soothing, then *RIP!* It hurt, but it was over quick. My skin would turn an angry shade of red, but it would eventually calm down.

The first time I had you waxed felt like a betrayal. No one

had told me how much it was going to hurt. I remember thinking that I must be a wimp because my friends weren't complaining about the pain. Do you remember the time I tried to take the waxing a step further and signed up for a bikini wax? Danger, danger, Eyebrows! Danger! It hurt so much I cried. Not snuffly little whimpers either, but full gasping sobs.

Finally, I gave threading, wicked threading, a go. The aesthetician wrapped individual hairs in thread and *ripped, ripped, ripped* until all your stray hairs were gone. The skin where you were was so angry it turned a deep magenta, and then broke out in tiny red bumps.

I'll never forget sitting in that chair, hands tightly gripping the chair arms, and panicking. I went into complete flight mode—racing heart, sweat in my palms, cold flooding my veins— but I forced myself to stay in the chair in an attempt to tame you, to make you shapely, to make you into something somebody else decided you should be. Cheesy love ballads were playing, and I remember thinking if I could just make it through the song, then the lady would be done. Oh, the irony of love ballads playing in the background while I hurt you. And I ignored the sadness I felt when I saw young girls waiting their turn for the torture.

Who decides what the perfect brow shape is? A fashion editor? A stepmom? An Instagram celebrity? I know your answer already—you decided when you began to grow.

Brows, why did I let other people dictate how you should look? Why did I let other people wound you into submission? Because the truth is, it wasn't just you being wounded into submission. I believed the lie that beauty equals pain. I signed us up to be hurt. I paid a lot of money to other people and gave them control over you and me.

The scariest thing is that once I started plotting your removal, I never questioned why I was removing you. I just agreed with a nebulous rule that it was a necessary part of my grooming, like showering. Even if it hurt.

So what changed my mind? I saw Taryn Brumfit's powerful documentary, *Embrace*. So many moments in the film struck a chord in me, but Harnaam Kaur inspired me. She's a beautiful young woman who lives with polycystic ovary syndrome, which causes her body to grow excessive facial hair. After enduring years of cruel bullying, she decided to stop removing her facial hair. She now lets her beard grow. I just remember thinking, *If that beautiful young woman can embrace her beard, then by God, I can embrace my eyebrows*. I made a promise to myself that I would never again pluck, wax, or thread another strand of you. And I haven't.

I'm sorry I hurt you. I won't do it again.

I have grown to love your wildness. It makes me chuckle to see you grow however you please. And you've added a white stripe for some additional flair. Thank you for teaching me that loving myself, loving my body, loving you doesn't mean conforming to anybody else's painful beauty expectations. No suffering necessary. You are beautiful just as you are.

Love, Me

Dear Taste Buds,

Remember eating lunch in the teachers' lounge during those early teaching days? And the assistant who always ate with us? One day she told me that she loved to watch me eat because I ate with gusto, that she could tell I really enjoyed my food.

You've always loved different flavors. I'm pretty sure you're among those super tasters who love the sweet and the sour and the salty and the spicy—you want all the flavors, and then you want more. I love that you live in such a wide-open way. Your curiosity has laid a path for me to experience pleasures and surprises almost anywhere I am. I love you for encouraging me to be more adventurous.

But I was embarrassed that day. Was she chastising or insulting me? Was I a pig at my trough? Was I too hungry? I thought she was poking fun at me, but now I think she was being sincere.

The truth is I *was* hungry. In the literal sense. I would be starving by the time lunch rolled around because it always took you some time to wake up, and food never tasted good to you in the mornings. So to taste the melding of flavors in my usual turkey sandwich brought me extra pleasure, an urge satisfied, comfort delivered to you. Even before your palate expanded to love all the green vegetables—brussels sprouts, even—medium-rare steak, cottage cheese, sushi, and red wine you used to think would be disgusting, you were so receptive to my bland offerings. You just wanted to embrace the flavors and squeeze every bit of joy out of them before I swallowed.

    I was hungry in a more ephemeral sense, too. I was starving to taste life. To know other cultures and countries, to see God, to have adventures. Growing up in a midsized Southern town the way we did left me yearning for the experiences I'd only read about, craving something more. Vacations happened only at the beach—the familiar tang of salt and sand a pleasure and comfort to you, despite the grit. Family meals and holidays were always at one of my grandmothers'—both excellent cooks. There are foods I associate with each of them—memories of tastes at their tables. What dish do you remember Mema making? For me, it's salads with every ingredient option diced in a separate bowl. Strawberry cakes. Sweet potato casserole with the crunchy pecan topping. Potato salad with paprika on top. Celery stuffed with pimento cheese. And Faye? It's fried chicken and red velvet cakes and baby biscuits and gravy.

    Going to college less than an hour away from home didn't expand our horizons as much as I'd expected it to, especially when I came home to visit so often. Seems I wanted familiarity more than adventure, despite what I told myself. The books I voraciously devoured were a safer way to experience the world. While I learned a lot of academic information and even a bit about other cultures, I didn't step far out of my comfort zone.

    I spent the bulk of my money on food, giving you sustenance and flavor. I had favorite dishes at local restaurants—*mmmm*, the turkey Reuben at Pot Belly Deli—and I frequented the grocery store often. I didn't cook a lot, but I made sure I had food you'd enjoy. Why didn't I save that money for a study-abroad experience, where you could sample new flavors foreign to us both?

When we moved to the "city"—small in the scale of cities and still Southern—after grad school, it felt like a grand adventure to pack up and move away from family. We were on our own to taste life. I loved to try new restaurants with you, but I lived with girls who didn't eat much of anything. Instead, we learned a lot about mixed drinks that would make the liquor more palatable. Again, I wonder why I spent so much money on drinks in local bars instead of more adventurous excursions.

My life felt small, my adventures small. But also safe. I judged myself. I worried that others would think I was ignorant, or worse, because of where and how I'd grown up, so I didn't put myself out there to be judged. But really, I was afraid to be seen, to live a vibrant, bold life, to break society's rules by being different. I had inklings that I didn't want the same bland experiences that I saw my peers having, but those little nudges scared me. If I stayed small and spent money on what I assumed everyone else was spending money on, then I would be safe. It was easier to numb myself with comfort foods and alcohol than to try something new, especially if I would be trying it alone.

Now I see that I was confused about how our "small" life could be rich. I wanted more, but I didn't spend the time to figure out what more meant. My way to change myself into a more sophisticated creature beyond judgment was to distance myself from the people and places I came from. Instead, I wasted a lot of time and money conforming to the new people around me rather than exploring what really moved me, what flavors excited you, what kind of life I wanted to live. Just as I did with Hair for so many years, I tried to jigsaw myself into groups rather than forging my own path and trusting I'd find myself and my people on the way.

Thankfully, our tastes have matured. I like to titillate you with new recipes and delight in your pleasure when they're tasty. And together, we've seen parts of the country and the world that have broadened us. We've survived and thrived while sampling spiky-skinned jackfruit and sucking the heads of crawfish and pickling giardiniera.

I've matured in other ways, too. I'm not as scared to step outside the lines anymore and choreograph my own dance. I don't have to play small to be safe. It's okay to let other people see what I really enjoy and what I really believe. The ones who aren't interested in the real me are free to go, and the folks who stick around will lift me up in ways I can't even imagine yet.

I'm still hungry for flavors I can't find here at home—to travel the world, sharing delicacies and strange concoctions with you—but not because I think those experiences will paint how others view me. Now, it's because I want to soak in the richness of different cultures, solely for me, to fill my mouth with tender bites of monchong or a sparkling summer sangria, to fill my soul with the beauty of the world's wonders and the people who share this planet with me.

I also crave the nostalgia of our childhood. I know you do, too. We let the old comforts soothe us, whether that's digging our fingers into a bag of McDonald's salt-gritty french fries or tasting the ocean's seawater seasoning every time I take a deep belly breath on the beach. I appreciate the family members who have found contentment living in the same place and eating the same foods their entire lives. Different and exotic doesn't mean better. It just means different.

Wanting to inhale life, to live as boldly as I can, to give you every flavor, doesn't mean we can't appreciate the comfortable simplicity of daily life. It's an and/both situation, not an either/or. I don't have anything to prove to anyone about my sophistication or my worth based on the international delights you have or have not experienced. We don't lack flavor in our life.

I love knowing you're an eager partner in my escapades, always willing to say yes to something new. Thank you for being excited for each new adventure and for still appreciating the old faithfuls. I'm finally at a place of balance. I can be hungry for more and satiated with what I have.

Love, Me

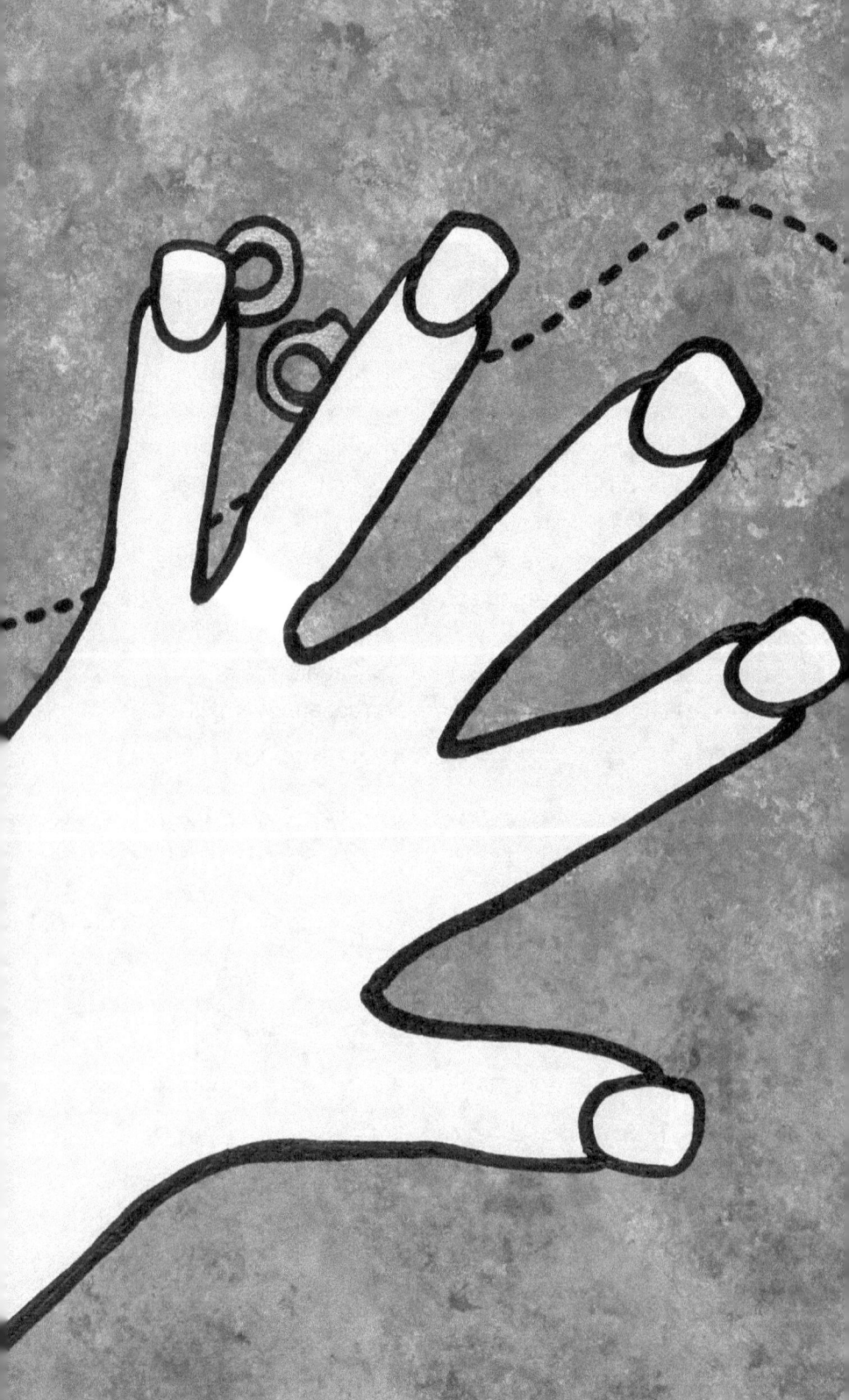

Dear Ring Finger on My Left Hand,

Thank you for supporting my marriage day after day, year after year. You have never balked at wearing my wedding band and engagement ring, despite their continued wear changing your shape and color. On the rare occasions that I take them off, I see the pale but luminous lines marking their spot, the curve inward as if you've been wearing a constrictive corset. Yet you don't seem to mind or feel caged. The symbols of the love Terry and I share have marked you as much as that love has changed me.

I think about what you represent—an outward acknowledgment of a promise I made to Terry. The permanent changes wrought in you remind me that my marriage isn't just a commitment to a man, but rather a commitment to the life and the family that we are creating together.

You always wanted to be marked as taken. You wanted the world to know that somebody chose you and made a promise to be with you always. You wanted to be loved. In the same way that books gave my taste buds grand ideas about the flavors of life, they gave you romantic notions about what love should be.

Our first relationship lasted six years, and you expected a diamond engagement ring. The next relationship lasted more than a year, and for a while, you were pretty sure he'd give you a ring eventually. Both times you were disappointed. I was too. It hurt to wonder when I would be loved enough for someone to commit to me forever and to secretly believe I wasn't worthy of that kind of fairy-tale love. Now, I look back in hindsight with so much gratitude that I didn't commit myself to those men, not because they did me wrong or they were weak, but because I wouldn't have known the expansiveness that loving Terry has created in my heart and life.

Finally, when the marriage proposal came, Terry didn't have a ring. All he had to offer was himself, which was such an abundant gift that neither of us really cared that there was no ring to wear. Funny now to think I told him to buy a washing machine instead! He didn't listen to me, obviously, or else this would be a different letter in a different book. "Dear Washing Machine" doesn't have the same feel, I must say.

When I reflect on those other relationships, I know we thought we wanted a ring. But what we really wanted was a family. A Beaver Cleaver family with a mom and a dad and brothers and sisters and a dog. All three men that I invested serious time in, including Terry, had that kind of family. The first two had families I adored. Their mothers were my confidantes, and their fathers were my buddies. They loved me almost as much as I loved them. They wanted me to be a part of their family. And I craved that normalcy. That Technicolor dream of the "perfect" family. Our own was so broken and lonely, with divorced parents who didn't tolerate each other's presence and no siblings to lean on when I was stuck in the middle. I thought I'd fill the holes with someone else's ready-made family.

I met Terry my very first night of college. We never dated or even hung out. He just always turned up in random places and moments. He'd say, "Hi, Bubbles." I'd cringe a bit when I heard the nickname I'd picked up that first night we met because of a goldfish T-shirt I was wearing, say hi back, and then move along. One night, a couple of years after college, he showed up in one of those random places, at one of those random moments, like the magical miracle he is, yelling, "Hey, Bubbles!" And our love story began.

While he loved me with his whole being, his mother did not. She didn't think I was the right choice for her son. I was a latchkey kid with divorced blue-collar parents, and while I wasn't particularly religious, I definitely was not Catholic. I had cut my teeth in the fire-and-brimstone, going-straight-to-hell version of Sunday school. How I wished for a personal history robust with culture to share when we met—those longings I shared with Taste Buds to be seen as worldly and sophisticated—so she'd think I was worthy of belonging to their family, that you were worthy to wear a ring gifted from Terry's heart.

For the first time, I had a man who loved me silly, but his mom showed me in a variety of ways, subtle and not so subtle, that I wasn't going to be easily accepted. Almost two decades later, I still catch my breath when I remember the night she made it clear she didn't think I'd be a good wife for Terry.

I'd been oblivious to the signals and subtle slights that could have clued me in sooner. Earlier that same day, when I'd shown her my wedding dress, I'd thought her lack of enthusiasm was because she didn't like my dress, not because she didn't like me. Maybe she thought we were playing at wedding planning, since you were still naked, and seeing my dress cemented it for her as a soon-to-be reality. Whatever her reasons, at dinner that evening, she bombarded me with poison-tipped questions I had no idea how to answer. I don't even remember all the specifics, but I do remember the sick wash of shame and fear that flooded my body. I felt exposed, as much a charlatan as the bonding that had covered my front tooth. Now Terry knew I wasn't good enough to love, much less to have you wear his engagement ring.

    The idea that she wouldn't like me was inconceivable. I'd cobbled together a fantasyland mother-in-law relationship, based on happy-family love stories in books and movies and previous experiences with ex-boyfriends' mothers, where she'd love me and we'd prepare family meals together and I'd have another mother to confide in and rely on. I was such a people-pleaser, always saying yes, wearing masks, contorting myself to make sure I was well received, especially by adults. Stop chuckling, I know I was an adult then, too, but being an adult didn't make me any less eager to please. I had a visceral need to be accepted, to be praised, to be good enough.

    And I wasn't. At least not to my future mother-in-law.

    My feelings were so hurt that I thought I might be physically wounded, my heart full of shrapnel, bleeding out. It was like every rejection I'd ever received coalesced into one explosive bomb. All these years later, I know it hurt so much because her acceptance mattered so much—I loved Terry. He was my person. He was my life partner.

He stepped into the fray that night, as did his sister, to protect me. He made it clear that he chose me, regardless of whether we had his mother's support or not. That was one of the times that his love was strong enough to carry me across the raging river of self-loathing and set me back on even ground.

Because I couldn't acknowledge how desperate I was to be seen as enough, as if others' validation would fill the hole that only I could fill with self-acceptance, I couldn't even begin to process that her feelings had nothing to do with me and everything to do with her. I had no idea what to do with my hurt, so I latched on to fury. That was much more palatable. And I suited up, piling on armor, so that even her apology couldn't get past my defenses. If she didn't want me, then I would reject her, too. Time dulled the pain, and distance made it easy to keep to myself, but every new perceived slight or criticism made the pain flare.

Our relationship mended, but it's never come close to that fantasyland façade I'd imagined. And I know that's mostly on me. I haven't been willing to brave that kind of vulnerability with her. But finally, I've begun to heal myself, to love myself, to recognize that I am enough and more, just like I am. Just recently, she told me she loved me, and I was able to receive it as the sincere gift it was intended as.

And I'm now so grateful for her initial rejection. It forced me to get very clear about the commitment I was making to Terry and why I was making it. For myself and no one else. For my heart and not a ring. For a lifetime and not a moment.

Ring Finger, we couldn't choose to wear Terry's ring because we loved his family. We had to choose to marry him because we loved *him*. We had to make our own family. That was how we needed to bind the wounds of our broken past and let them heal.

We could make our own version of Beaver Cleaver's family without the high heels and "yes, dears." We could decide what family meals and bedtime routines and everyday chores looked like with a committed partner because Terry was the balm we needed. I didn't have to crowbar myself into someone else's family to experience loving stability. We were free to dream wild dreams for our family while he kept our feet on the ground until we reversed roles. But always, we're together in our dreams.

I chose him. I still choose him. Every day. And you remind me with your band of radiant support that he was and is my first choice.

Love, Me

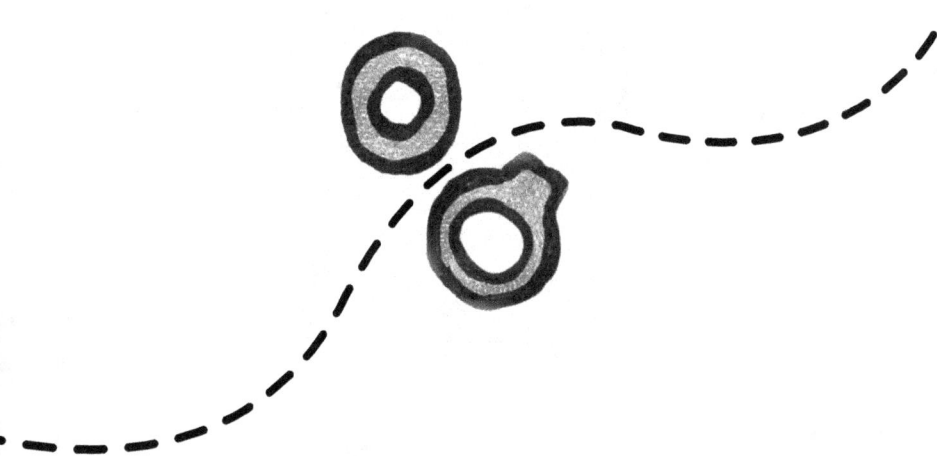

Dear Birthmark,

My mom said that I was born with you, that you were like the birthmark that all babies in our family have been born with—a red ragged-edged circle on the backs of all our heads. I recently read that some people call you a stork bite. While I don't remember ever seeing you on my own head, I did get to see you on both of my daughters. What magical matriarch placed her palm on her baby's head, marking her as her own, passing her lineage on to each new generation?

I share many physical traits with my maternal family, everything from my mom's shape to our hazel-green eye color. But I've spent most of my life feeling like a cabbage-patch baby all the same. I just don't seem to fit in with my family—never have. It's like looking in a funhouse mirror. I see our resemblances, but I can't make them add up with my feelings of disconnection.

These physical commonalities, including you, Birthmark, don't translate into other familial connections. As a little girl, I read books instead of playing outside, and I found most of my self-worth in being good and making straight A's. I studied theater in high school and moved away from the town where they've all found contentment. I lean pretty far left, and I don't own a gun. I don't meet God the same way most of them do. I don't iron jeans or wear high heels. I wear my feelings on my face. None of this means much of anything, except I've always had a hard time connecting with them in meaningful ways. How can I look like I belong in this family on the outside when nothing on the inside seems to fit?

The only member on our maternal side I regularly talk to is my grandmother, but when I go for visits, everyone else is kind and always seems genuinely glad to see me. I know they're proud of me and my accomplishments—they've shown up for the important events in my life, given me thoughtful gifts, and shared their good wishes with me. I even believe them when they tell me they love me. They did their best by me as I grew up. But I do sometimes wonder if they just love me because I am family. Birthmark, did you create a familial obligation to love me because you marked me as one of them? Would they still love me if you didn't exist, if we weren't related? Because I don't think they know the real me—I keep her hidden around them.

I always feel like an odd bird when I visit. As Taste Buds know so well, I itch to travel to foreign lands. I consume as many books as I can get my hands on. I eat sushi. Sometimes I see an inkling of something in an uncle or a cousin and wonder if there—right there—is where we can connect, dig deeper than surface level, and talk about something with substance. But then that spark winks out, usually because I said more than they wanted to hear or asked a question they didn't want to answer or vice versa.

I think they've judged me as too sensitive or too nerdy or too arrogant or too different or too high-falutin' or just plain too much my whole life. The maternal relatives I've felt closest to were aunts by marriage. When I was growing up, they seemed to understand me in a way that my blood relatives never have or never wanted to.

And truth be told, I don't know my relatives either. I don't know what they love the most. Or what keeps them up late at night. I've made assumptions about them—some based in my personal experiences, others on their Facebook posts. I've kept my distance.

But, Birthmark, you've marked me as related to them. What connects me to these strangers also known as my family? What's my purpose here?

I think maybe I was born to be different, so I could dismantle some generational bondage. The women in my maternal family—including me—have struggled with perfectionism issues for as far back as I can tell. We worry about how we look, about how our homes look, about how we'll be perceived by others, and if we think it will be less than perfect, then we get to work making things just so in order to change the narrative. My grandmother used to joke that she kept a pair of clean panties in her glovebox in case she had a car accident and needed a new pair. As if there would be a moment she could pause the chaos and make herself presentable for the emergency workers. Company, even family, was never allowed to visit without making the house spit-shine clean first. And messy feelings were hidden behind a veneer of smiles and invisible armor. Ask Front Tooth about her experience with those false facades.

I'm done living that way. I will have crazy eyebrows and a round tummy and funky hair, and I will revel in what makes me unique. I have dropped the heavy bag of "should" I carried around for much too long. I don't make decisions based on what I believe others will think of me anymore. I'm practicing the notion that done is better than perfect and that the best way to learn is to screw up. I'm not hiding my light until I get my messaging perfect, and if someone shows up at my house unannounced, I guarantee you that there will be dog hair on the rug and dirty dishes in the sink. I might even still be in my pajamas. And I don't care. This is who I am. I love my imperfect self, especially my sweet front tooth with the teeny chip. I'm finally free of being perfect, so I can accept and love myself.

Birthmark, you're covered by Hair, and I imagine you've faded as we've aged, the same way the strawberry birthmark above my left nipple did. I'm fascinated by you, though. This connection to family, many of whom I don't even know names of, from generations back. I'm curious about who my people were. And when I saw the red mark on both of my daughters, I wanted to pluck that string tying all of us together. I wanted to know just who we come from. Would she want to know me? Would I belong with her? Would I be welcome just like I am?

I like to think she'd hug me tight, offer me something to eat and drink, and sit me down to tell me just how loved I am.

Love, Me

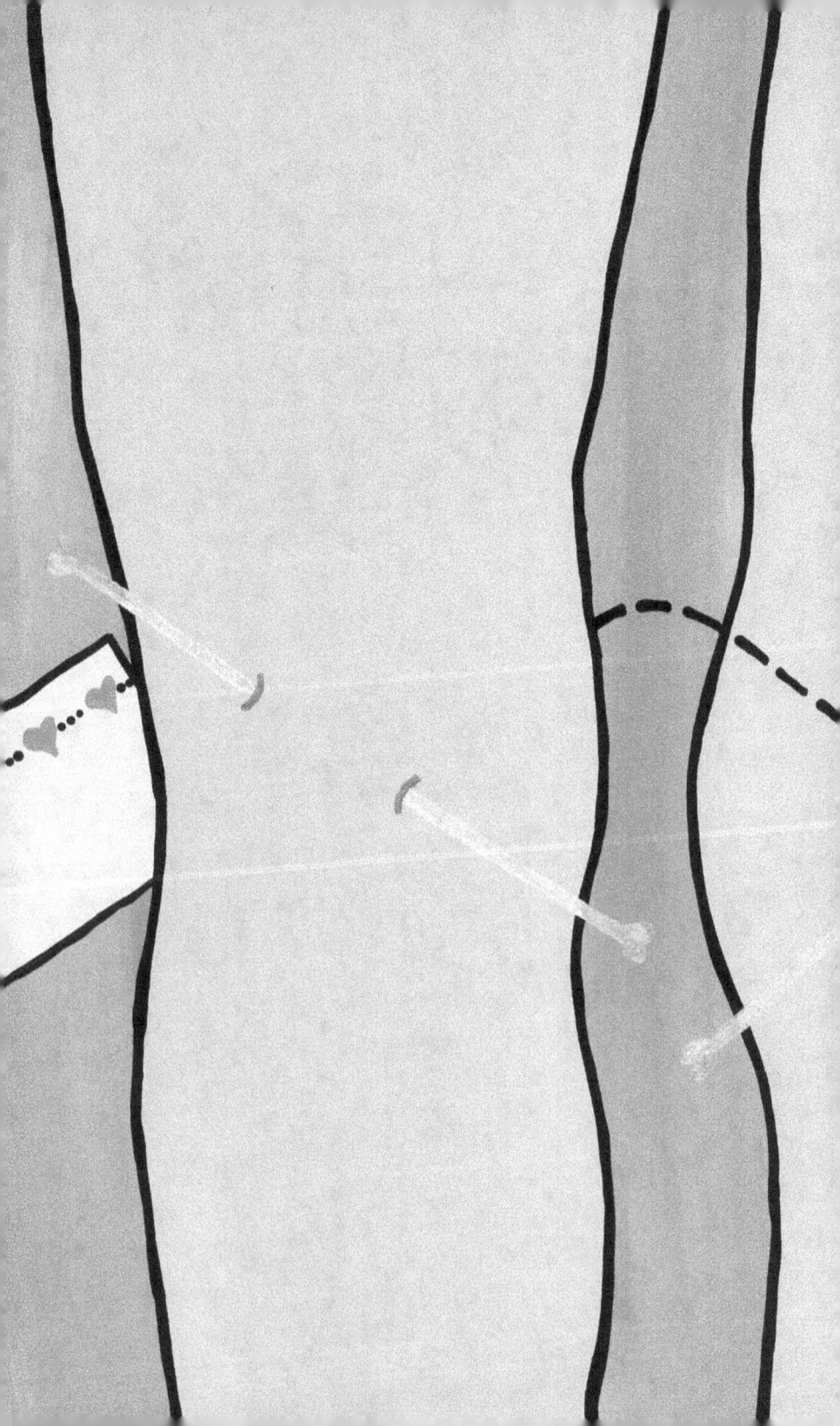

Dear Knees,

Thank you for bending and straightening, bending and straightening, bending and straightening—with ease and through pain. Thank you for the many times you've healed and for welcoming extra hardware and Cadaver Bone to keep me in motion. Thank you for your strong support.

I used to say you were weak. That you made *me* weak. I believed you were bad, biological defects that I was forced to live with, and I used you as an excuse when I was afraid to challenge myself physically. Four surgeries for a woman in her early forties, who wasn't a serious athlete—okay, who wasn't an athlete at all—is unusual. A curiosity. People want to know what our scars are about, or why we're not into skiing, or the root cause of your issues. As if they can ward against the cooties if they have the magic phrase. I hated that your scars garnered attention, that your brokenness forced me to depend on other people for help.

My parents always met my basic needs, but from a very early age, I believed I had to rely on myself. I was a surprise baby, unexpected, and if I'm being brutally honest, I'm sure unwanted, too. I get it. My parents were teenagers still in high school. I have so much gratitude for them, because even though they hadn't wanted a baby when they were still babies themselves, they provided for me with their very best. I grew up being told how loved I was when I was born, the implication (in my mind) that I wasn't loved before birth. While I was often cherished, I also intuitively knew that my existence was sometimes an imposition, a resentment. Adult me completely understands those feelings, but little-girl me felt guilty for derailing their lives. She just wanted to be loved.

    I became fiercely independent and capable so that I wouldn't be a bother. The less burdensome I was, the more likely I'd be wanted. As I grew, without the ability to articulate these complex feelings, I began to hide behind my armor. Terry has teased me that he can tell when I'm feeling particularly vulnerable because I suit up like Iron Man. It's such an apt metaphor for how I feel inside: I don't need any help. I will do everything myself. I'm the only one I can rely on.

    The paradox is that, as a child, I craved someone to help me navigate my homework and physical therapy and college applications. And as an adult, I crave close relationships with people who will help me when life shows up to smack me down, or who will celebrate with me when life is sweet. But I was (and sometimes still am) afraid to ask for help and be rejected. When someone asks me how they can help me, I rarely have an answer. My mind just blanks, as if I can't comprehend how to receive. Knees, as you bore the weight of my body, you also bore the heavy responsibility and isolation of my self-reliance.

    Is that why you were injured? So that I would be forced to lean on my parents? And friends? And strangers? Do you think that's also why my cervix forced me on bedrest when I was pregnant with Campbell, so I'd have to depend on Terry and coworkers and family?

Knees, you showed me that I'm not alone, that help is always there if I just ask for it. Because I had no choice but to ask for help when you were injured. Going to prom on crutches and starting grad school in a wheelchair on a hilly campus forced me to admit I was vulnerable.

I'm laughing and crying at my stubbornness in hindsight. I wish I had learned the lesson you were trying to show me the first time you were injured—that I am worthy of receiving every good thing. I am not a burden. I will be loved even when I'm needy. I wish I didn't have to learn so many lessons the hard way. I imagine you wish that, too.

But I think I've got it now. Last year, when we took the girls camping in the Everglade wilds, I tripped and you twisted and I fell. You tried so hard to keep me upright, but you couldn't. You had to let me fall one more time so that I could finally realize that I am fully supported. I'm not alone. I can be vulnerable and receive love and care.

I was so sad and hurt and embarrassed that I couldn't play a simple game with my family without falling and getting hurt. I put myself to bed in my hammock and cried quietly because I was so tired of you failing me. Terry came to check on me and, in the most loving way, reassured me that he would always be with me, taking care of me, pushing my wheelchair or carrying my cane if that's what I needed. I finally believed him. And I trust that if we're both in wheelchairs that God will provide the perfect people to push us. Maybe those two beautiful souls we've helped create. Or better yet, we'll get the motorized versions and race each other.

We've been through a lot, Knees, you and me.

You haven't failed me. I haven't failed me. God hasn't failed me. You've shown me that it's safe to trust. Someone will always be there to pick me up when I fall.

Love, Me

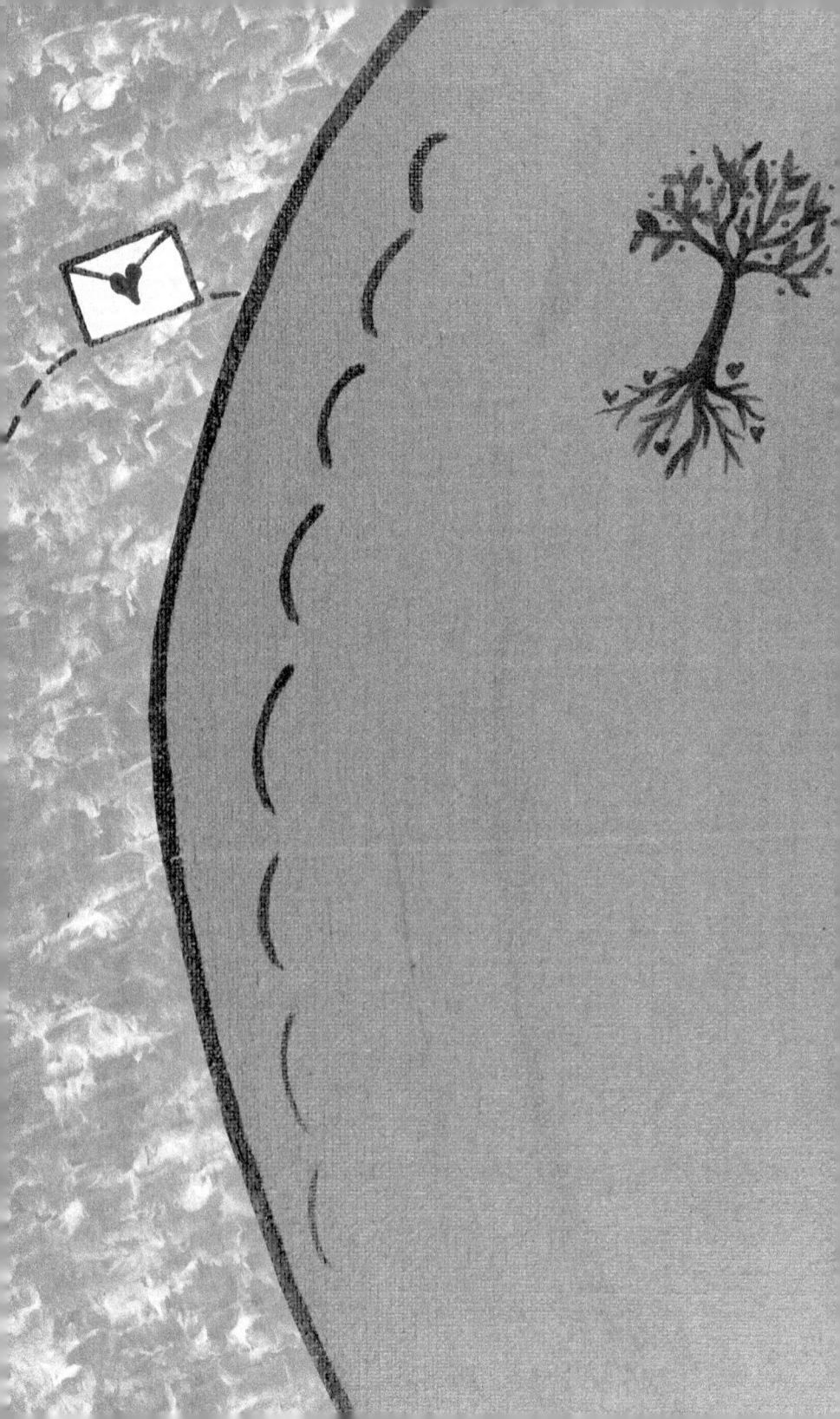

Dear Back,

Thank you for trying to keep me in check. It's as if I can't see how hard I'm being on myself until you start aching. I get heartburn when I expect myself to do everything, to get it done right away, and to make sure the delivery is perfect. I get constipated when the stress of not being able to do everything immediately and the pain of perfectionism creeps in. And you, Back, you hurt for the same reasons.

I remember the first time you felt crippled with pain that radiated from my right butt cheek and into my hip, up to your lower-right side. We had been relegated to bedrest during my pregnancy with Campbell, which meant I sat or laid down all the time—for three months. You began to throb and ache, and sometimes the pain would be so intense I would want to claw my skin to create a distraction. I felt like I was failing at being the picture-perfect pregnant mama.

You're aching in the same spot now—I've been writing too long in my office chair. Long car rides hurt you, too.

And your pain is so easy to stave off or to ease. All I need to do is get up and move frequently, to stretch, to offer myself respite. Yet I don't. I force myself to meet unrealistic deadlines that I've set for myself, waiting until you ache to realize I need to get up and move. I'll use an app to remind me for a while, and then I fall back into my old habits when I feel like I'm running behind or that I can't get everything done without sacrificing you to the pain.

Sadly, I thought being a loving mother also meant you had to ache. I carried both of my babies a lot, but especially Jude. She didn't walk until she was eighteen months old, and she loved to be held close to me. Pain would flare in your left shoulder blade, and rather than putting her down and beginning the work of teaching her about boundaries, I would grimace through it until I was near tears. How could I teach her boundaries when I didn't hold any?

The harder I tried to be a perfect mother, to get all the things right, the more pain you experienced. When Boobs couldn't carry the weight of my expectations alone, you supported them. My god, I feel vestiges of it now, remembering those days, remnants of wanting to control my relationships with the girls, to make them strong, our bond unbreakable, all the while ignoring that I was breaking myself.

When you hurt, I'm hurting myself. I'm working too many hours, carrying too many loads of "should," saying yes when what I meant was no. When you hurt, I'm being especially hard on myself. I'm not holding boundaries. I'm not loving you.

I know, then, it's time to start over. Again. To stretch you with yoga poses, like bridges and camels and forward folds. To take breaks while I work and to set fluid deadlines because things always come up. It's time to visit the chiropractor on a regular basis and schedule monthly massages. To be gentle and forgiving with myself for losing sight of my boundaries so many times. You're faithful to keep showing me. I want to transmute your pain into a neon billboard with flashing lights and whirligigs: Nicole, love yourself. Take care of yourself. Hold your boundaries.

I love you, Back. I don't want to wait to show you I love you only when you feel paralyzed with pain. I want to love you consistently, not because you're hurting, but because you're an integral part of me. You're so strong, often carrying me, pushing me forward, leaving behind what I don't need, offering your protection from the storms that come.

I want to indulge you in the tickly back rubs I loved as a little girl. I want to support you as you support me. I want to enjoy life with a pain-free you.

As the part of me that represents my past, I know you're a treasure trove of wisdom I can pull from. Thank you for your integrity to stand tall and teach me what I need to know, as many times as I need to hear your message until I get it.

Love, Me

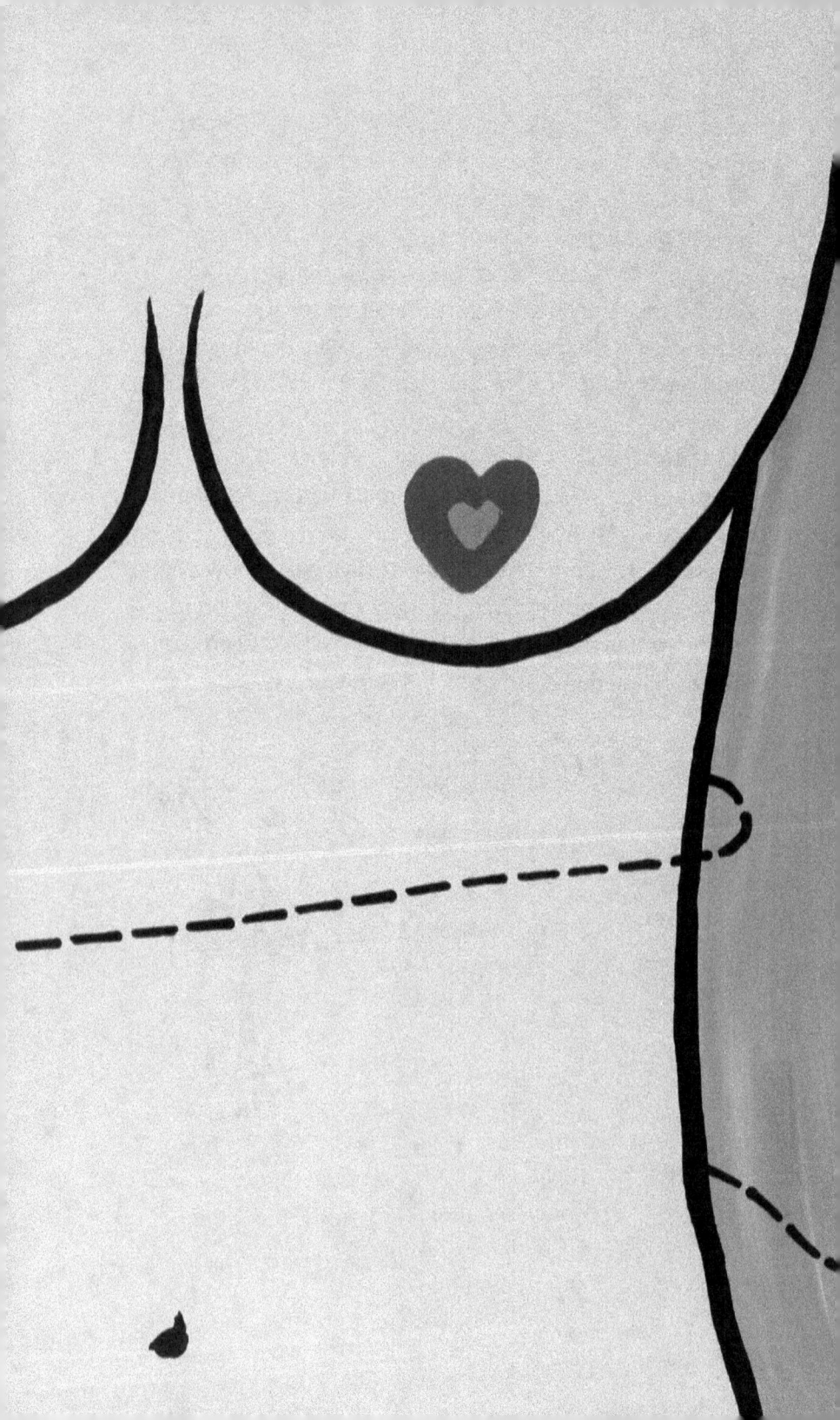

Dear Boobs,

We have some history, me and you. I remember being titillated and ashamed of you during early adolescence. You grew at a rate that I didn't know what to do with. And while I sort of liked the new attention that came when you showed up—a full C-cup, no less—I also sort of hated the weirdness of being compared and objectified. You were too much.

I loved your curves, your sensuality, the softness when I touched you. Glimpsing a peek of you in a V-necked tee made me smile with secret desire. And yet, with you filling out a C-cup, the rest of me was round, too: tummy, hips, butt, thighs. That didn't feel acceptable. Your loveliness was not enough to convince me that all my round, ripe curves could be cherished. I was willing to lose your cleavage rather than be round everywhere else. You were not enough.

Your bodaciousness lured in men much older than me, who would stare, and boys my own age, who would dare each other to pop my bra. You were too big to hide, so I had to learn how to navigate the world while receiving unwanted attention. Remember, in high school, when I was playing the role of a baby angel in *The Best Christmas Pageant Ever,* and I bound you with an Ace bandage? That was uncomfortable. And fruitless. You were too much.

Later, when Campbell was born, you never fed her enough. I was so angry with you (and me). I felt like such a loser. Why couldn't I feed my child? Why weren't you making milk? What was wrong with you? Why were you shrinking when you were supposed to be bursting with milky goodness? (Never mind that I was counting food points and pushing myself to be thin.) You were not enough.

With Jude, I couldn't stop you from nursing. Milk spewed out of you all the time. There was no way to predict when you'd leak. And just wait until I got into the shower. You squirted milk like Bessie in the pasture. For an entire year, you were Jude's sole milk source. It was like you were saying you were sorry for being less than with Campbell and you overcompensated with Jude. I couldn't get space to breathe, and I was angry with you again. Why was I the only one who could feed my child? Why were you making so much milk? What was wrong with you? You were too much.

Too much. Not enough. Too much. Not enough. Too much. Not enough.

This is a litany of lies I believed for too many years. Not just about you, Boobs, but about all of me. The narration was uneven, of course. My body was almost always too much, too big, too fat. A teenage boy called me Hogatha once. You better believe that got stuck on repeat. But my work, whatever I was trying to accomplish, was never enough. I didn't measure up. I didn't work hard enough. I should have done more.

The work of untangling those lies is arduous. Just when I think I've cleared out all the webs, I'll run smack into a dusty corner I wasn't expecting to find. Motherhood is a particularly tender path.

I worry about what messages I passed to my sweet babies as you fed them. Campbell, you're not enough. Jude, you're too much. Lest you think I'm a paranoid mother, I see them playing these lies out. Campbell won't be satisfied with less than an A, as if she's not enough otherwise. Jude hides under tables when she thinks she's too emotional. Oh god, Boobs, in my efforts to chastise you into being "just right," I think I've passed on a load of bullshit to my girls.

It's like the label of mother comes packaged with so many expectations that I'll never meet them all. Whose expectations am I talking about? Society's certainly. Social media's. The authors' of the parenting books. The stranger staring at me in the restaurant, store, airport. Friends' and family's, of course. Terry's. Campbell's and Jude's. And the most insidious of all, my own.

I began to try on these expectations even before I was pregnant, when I judged my mother and mother-in-law and how they mothered and evaluated whether it matched how I wanted to mother or not.

I want to be the mom Campbell and Jude confide in, the mom who makes homemade organic meals with ingredients from her garden, the mom who has a clean house and all the laundry put away, the mom who always welcomes their friends, the mom who models how to have a servant's heart and an activist's fire, the mom who's a soft place to land (that's where you come in, Boobs), the mom who still romances their dad (there's a role for you here, too, Boobs), the mom who earns her own money and runs her own business, the mom who creates magic with her words, the mom who takes care of herself but who also takes care of them and meets everyone's needs all of the time in the most perfect ways.

Often the ugly little voice in my head whispers that I've cocked it up again. I gave Jude too much advice about how she could have handled the mean girl on the bus when all she wanted me to do was listen. Or I'm so wrapped up in my phone that I missed half of what Campbell shared about her day. Or I bust my tail to make Christmas spectacular, doing too much, more than I want to, only to feel like it's not enough when their reactions don't meet my expectations.

Why am I so hard on myself, and why do I wage this battle between not being enough or being too much around my mothering? I love my daughters so much. I want to give them the Baby Bear experience of everything being "just right," as opposed to the never-satisfied Goldilocks.

But the truth is, I can't control their experiences. They are already their own selves with their own desires and needs and perceptions. No matter my best intentions, sometimes I'll hit the right note with them, and other days I'll screw up badly and need to apologize. I can only show up as I am, releasing all the expectations I cling to in order to prove myself a good mother. I'm already a good mother—there was never a question—doing the best I can with what I have in any given moment.

Boobs, you aren't nursing my daughters anymore, but those many months you spent nourishing them established an unbreakable bond between us. I have faith that your hard work wasn't in vain. That I have a chance to help them know the truth about themselves now, not years from now.

They are enough just exactly like they are, regardless of the expectations surrounding them, be it their own or someone else's. And I can show them my truth: I am enough just exactly like I am.

And Boobs, dear Boobs, you are enough, too. Your cup size, your milk production, your perkiness, your cleavage, your sensuality, your everything is just right. In fact, I think you are pretty damn amazing.

Love, Me

Dear Tear Factory,

I'm sorry I've always been ashamed of you. The tears you generate come with their own mess: a splotchy red face, snot, and feelings. I didn't want to be perceived as weak, especially when I was angry or hurting. Those feelings had already made me too vulnerable. Your tears' arrival was more than I could bear.

When I was little, my family thought I was sensitive. I was. I sobbed during my first movie, *The Fox and the Hound*. And my second movie, *Annie*. And my third, *E.T.* You cranked up production at the first sign I'd disappointed an adult. I even went through a fearful phase in first grade, where I tried to run away from school, because I couldn't hold your tears in. My first-grade teacher had made it abundantly clear that tears were not allowed the day I cried because she spanked a boy who'd dared to throw up in her classroom. In my attempt to be perfect and hold back your easily flowing tears, I think I had a first grader's version of a panic attack.

I internalized contradictory messages about my sensitivity from the grown-ups around me. It was precious when I cried about a man experiencing homelessness and worried about where he'd sleep or what he'd eat. It was sweet when I couldn't finish *Where the Red Fern Grows* because I couldn't see the words for the tears dripping on the page. I was tenderhearted.

Nicole C. Ayers

But it was annoying when I cried because I'd spilled chocolate milk on our coffee table. It was frustrating when an adult's reprimand flooded me with remorse and tears. It was even angering when I cried for a doll in Sky City. Those tears showed me a spanking would follow that sort of emotional display. So what I internalized was that it was okay to cry for other people, but not for myself.

My parents were mostly flummoxed about what to do with my sensitive soul. Were they supposed to let me cry? Tell me to suck it up? Talk to me about my feelings? They were so young that I can't imagine they knew what to do. I'm raising a sensitive soul, too, and there are so many times I'm at a loss as to what to do for her. But I've made her a promise that we'll figure it out together. And when I take time to pause, I remember that I don't need to do anything *for* her. Her feelings are her own. All I need to do is show up and be *with* her when they become overwhelming and model healthy strategies to feel all our feelings. I don't want either of my girls to learn my own jacked-up strategies, which were to stuff my feelings down, hide your tears, or apologize every time I was emotional. I can't count the times I've literally hidden in my closet so I could cry without anyone knowing because I didn't feel safe to share my anger or grief or hurt. That would have made me feel much too vulnerable, and for so long, I viewed vulnerability as a weakness.

It is time I stop caring that your tears make others uncomfortable. Red Boot Way meetings taught me the beauty of letting myself cry without excuse or apology by sitting with other people who needed to cry without expecting an excuse or an apology for my discomfort. I've learned to get my own tissues when I need them and to let you fall when I don't and to ask for comfort when that will soothe me best.

    Your tears live so close to the surface, and they are welcome here. There is so much beauty in the world. Books and movies trigger your production factory often. And watching almost any athletic endeavor, from a child's soccer game to an Olympic medal event, makes me cry. There's something so poignant about watching a human give their best effort in front of others. Glimpsing random acts of kindness between strangers also touches me in a deep heart place.

    These days, I also cry when I experience tender moments with Campbell, Jude, and Terry. I cry tears of truth when I experience a goose-bump awareness that something was meant for me, such as a song or a quote, or I receive confirmation that my intuition is trustworthy. I cry with grief and then joy and pride when I have an epiphany that lets me heal my wounds.

    You provide me with a release that is so cleansing. When my heart is bursting with love, your prickling allows me to release the overflow in my heart. I treasure that I'm sensitive to the hard work of others, and I hope it always makes me cry.

    Your tears help me connect to loved ones, strangers, and sometimes fictional souls even, with empathy and love. Your tears show up when my passion rises to remind me what's important. You allow me to feel rage and express it without wounding others. And when I feel broken, you help me surrender my grief. Tears cleanse me again and again. I love you for making me a badass crier. Warrior on!

Love, Me

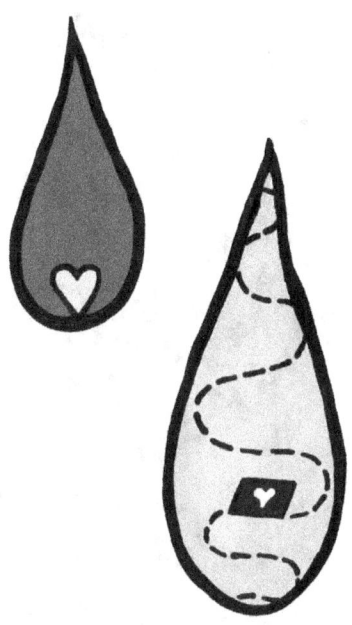

Dear Hands,

There's this nodule, a strange little growth in your left palm, that is giving me pause. It just appeared one day, but I didn't notice it until you were clapping and I felt discomfort. Pain feels like too strong a word, but the truth is, it hurt. I wonder if that bump formed one of the many times when I gripped you so tightly, trying to control my life. Or did it form slowly over the years, the way a pearl forms in an oyster, a tiny irritation that thrives under pressure?

That idea resonates with me. How about with you? Have I created a pearl of armor in my attempts to protect myself? God knows I've spent most of my life trying to control everything so that I could trick myself into feeling safe. I've hung on so tightly to rules and ideas and opinions and finances and grades and tests and my children's behavior and my relationships and my beliefs about God and my health . . . and . . . and . . . and . . .

I've clung to notions as if I can micromanage my way to success. I make assumptions about how others will perceive me if I say no or fall short or step outside the lines or disappoint them. And forget leaning on anybody else for help. Right, Knees? I keep such a tight grip I can't let go to grab a lifeline or a helping hand. Because then I wouldn't look like I could do it all. I would be vulnerable.

Are you okay?

I'm sorry if my inability to let go has left you hurting. I'm changing. Brené Brown's work around vulnerability has been showing me that I can dare greatly, especially in the intimacy of my closest relationships. Elizabeth Dialto's Wild Soul Movement has been teaching me to trust myself and my body. Working with Marni, an intuitive healer, has blessed me with the gifts of looking inward, of loving myself more, of releasing the weights I no longer need to carry. And I read a book recently, Tosha Silver's *Outrageous Openness*, that left me reeling in joy and wonder. I've been looking for magical miracles ever since. I'm learning that if I walk around with you wide open, I'm going to be okay. I'm going to be better than okay. I'm going to be safe and loved and delighted.

    I think there's room for you to heal yourself (and me). Is it possible to deconstruct a pearl? I'm going to trust you to find the answer. When I choose to let you go, without trying to make things "just so," I feel the tension leave you.

    You find joy in tapping, tapping, tapping on the keyboard, stringing words together from my heart. It's like the two of you have a direct connection. When I get out of your way, you flow. Remember winning the keyboarding award in high school? Learning to type without looking at you meant I had to trust you. You were showing me then that exciting things could happen if I just focused on staying present in the moment and didn't worry about the end result. I wish I had realized how magical you were back then. You are trustworthy.

    You surprised me with the joy you found molding wet clay into a serving bowl and throwing smaller ramekins on the pottery wheel. The heat of friction between you and the clay as the wheel spun allowed me to be so present that, again, we had no room to control the outcome. You are trustworthy.

And you've shown me your strength and capability to bear my weight as I learned how to do a handstand, something I never thought I could do. There's a moment right before I flip upside down, when I'm afraid every single time. But I raise you high, squeeze you into fists of courage, and then release you. I know you'll catch me again. You balance me right on the edge, hold me aloft, and then gently put my feet back on the ground. I don't have to try so hard. I just have to stay present. You are trustworthy.

You know how to hold dear ones—babies, my lover, books, colorful felt pens—without breaking them. You know when to squeeze a hand closer, and you know when it's time to release a connection. You are trustworthy.

It's time for me to relinquish the fears that tell me I need control, to dive deep into the wonder of life, trusting that you've got me every step of the way. I will drop my armor and walk my path with you, both of us open to receive blessings.

Love, Me

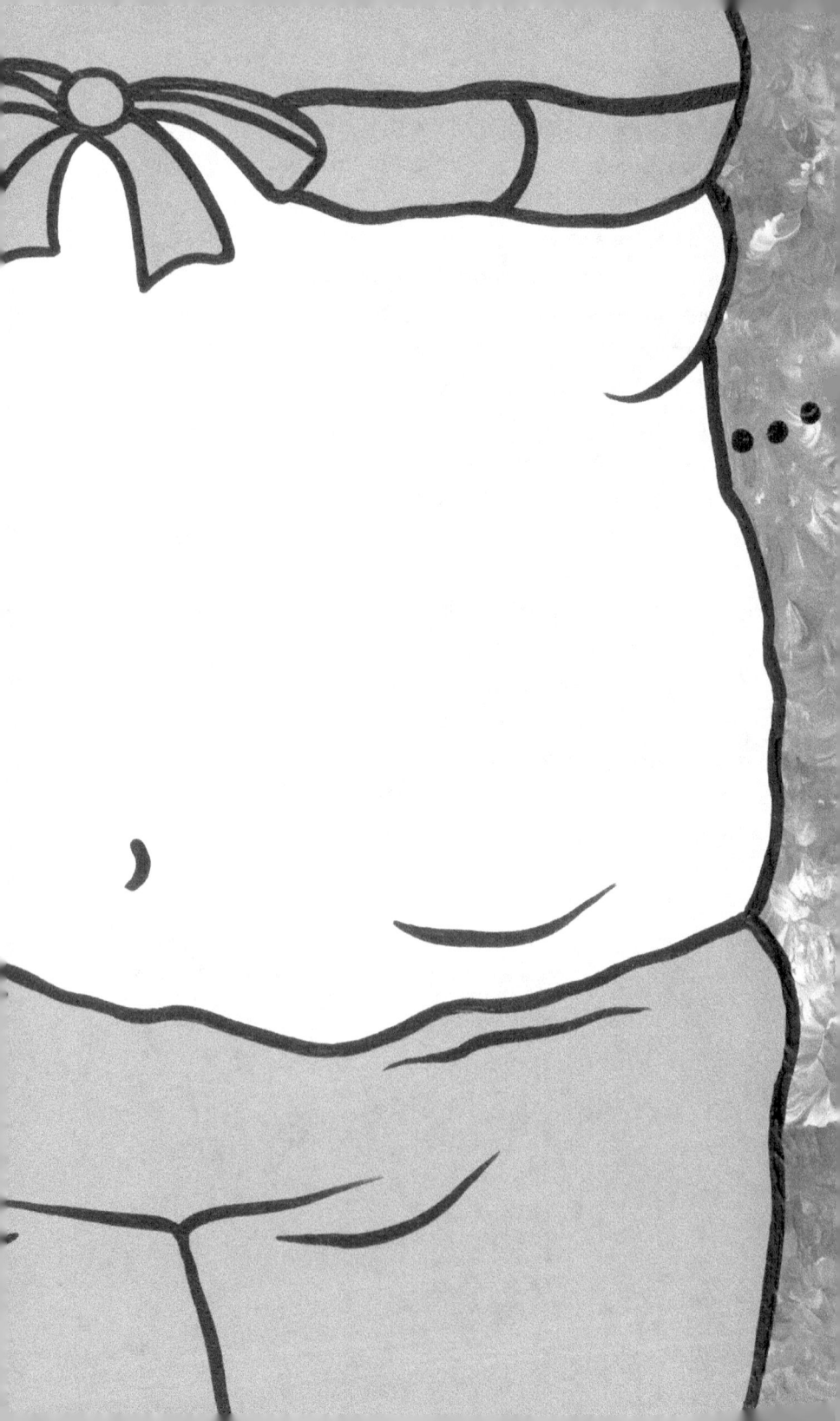

Dear Belly,

You symbolize the contradiction of body love and hate I've carried around my entire life, all centered around my weight. The juxtaposition of love and hate creates confusion and chaos. There's no way to move forward when you're always at odds.

Do I love you? Yes, yes, I do. You hold so many systems dear. You turn my food into nutrition my body needs. You remove toxins and waste that harm me. You grew and stretched with my babies—god, it was so easy to love you when they lived inside you. I could see your glorious bounty of skin and thrill at you. I wanted to touch you all the time. I loved you so.

And now, I touch you and feel your softness, your fullness, your capacity for creation, and I feel awe.

Do I hate you? Yes, yes, I do. Sometimes. I see a photo of your rolls or a side angle of you in the mirror, and my first reaction is to cringe. I think you're too fat, too full, too pregnant-looking. I just want you to disappear. I ignore you or camouflage you or Spanx you to pretend you're something that you're not.

I see your roundness as a weakness. I lie and tell myself I don't have a strong core, even though I'm great at balancing my body in yoga poses and handstands and on paddleboards.

I'm aware of the crazy-making thought patterns

that lead me to negative thoughts of you. I have been conditioned since birth to believe that thin bodies are beautiful, that flat is where it's at when it comes to you, but you've never been thin, even when the rest of me was. You've always had a little pooch of softness. And just like many of the other knots I've been untangling, I refuse to believe any longer that women must look like Stepford wives to be beautiful.

I can see how confused you must feel. You must wonder if I love you unconditionally, just as you are, with no judgment, or if I need you to conform, to slim down, before I can let my love flow through you.

Here's the thing: I do love you. I love you. I love you.

It's time to accept you as you are, to accept what I can't or won't change. I have a curvy body, and I can't change that. Not without surgery anyway. I've already had seven surgeries, two of which were C-sections you had to heal from, which is a gracious plenty, so I'm never going to elect to have a tummy tuck. Also, I like feeling softness in my breasts and butt and hips. And if those body parts are soft, you're going to be soft, too.

And I've decided I don't want to restrict myself to low-calorie foods or count points so you'll shrink. I love food, as do Taste Buds. I don't want to deprive myself or think about whether a food is allowed or healthy; I just want to eat whatever my body craves. Some days that's green smoothies and salads and garlicky quinoa. And sometimes I want to indulge in sweets and booze and fast food without feeling like I must punish myself later.

I want to move my body in juicy stretches and funky dances and long walks. I don't want to hold planks for an eternity or compress myself into tight crunches to try and change your shape. I want to move because it feels good, not because I want you to be something you're not.

How can I show you I fully accept you just as you are?

I can touch you with love, grasping your curves in my hands and cherishing the solidity of you. I can giggle when you jiggle. I can wear clothes that don't fetter you into constricted places. I can stop sucking you in. I can let the sun shine on you. It's been a long time since I wore a bikini, but I miss those days. Maybe I'll give it a whirl next summer.

I can stop cringing when I see pictures of you.

In reality, I know this won't change right away. I have to keep breaking the chain of lies that says fat is ugly or bad or something to hide. Every time I cringe, I can remind myself I no longer believe that about you. I can cherish your pregnant-like fullness because I know you are the sacred place where I create magic in this world. I can be grateful for the space you helped me fill when I needed more room to feel safer in this world so that I could face the demons of my past. I can be inspired by your food-magic chemistry as you process food into nourishment for every part of my body and rid yourself of the toxins I no longer need. I can celebrate your inner strength as you balance my body in new ways.

I love you, Belly. I love your innie. I love your soft roundness. I love you. And I am committed to staying on this journey of acceptance with you for the rest of our lives.

Love, Me

Dear Body Parts I Haven't Written To (Yet),

While this list is long, you are all important to me. You are loved for being a part of me. Some of you don't care to be recognized. Others are like, "Hey, what about me?" And a few of you are clamoring for my attention.

I see you: Vagina, Skin, Heart, Brain, Cervix, Thyroid. I hear you. I think about you often.

Vagina, you and I are healing some old, deep wounds. Our story is too tender to invite anyone else to read. Part of our healing has been to discern that I'm not ready to share our experiences. I'm comfortable protecting you from any readers' expectations that your story be included. This time, my no means no, and I can and will protect you. Maybe there will come a time when I do want to share the love letters I've written you, but it's okay that now is not that time.

Skin, I don't even know where to begin with you. I've just started to unpack your whiteness and the privileges I hold because of it, as well as the harm I've caused because of it. It would be irresponsible to share our journey when we are just diving into what your whiteness means. We have a lot of work to do. And there are voices of color we need to be listening to.

And you, Cervix, I'm just not there. I love you as a part of me, I do. But I'm still creeping my way toward forgiving you. I don't understand why you began to open so early with Campbell, sending me into preterm labor, endangering my baby, and sidelining me on bedrest for three months. You made me feel like a failure as a mother before I even had a baby to hold in my arms. I'm pissed, even though I've mined a few of your lessons already. I'm just not ready to fully forgive and accept you yet. And that's okay.

    Thyroid, you gave me my first close-up look at my own mortality when I found out you were covered in nodules. All benign, thank God! But still so scary to contemplate. I know there is work to do with you, but it hasn't surfaced yet. I'll be here when it does.

    Heart and Brain, you are treasures to me. I feel that I could write volumes to you as I plumb your depths. I love the anticipation of writing letters to you that will reveal so many insights into me. Your letters are coming, I promise.

    Precious body parts of mine, our friendship, our relationship, our love story is just beginning. I'll be here for all of it.

Love, Me

Acknowledgments

My Deepest Gratitude

To my Divi, for your providence in the creation of this book, in the creation of my life.

To my sisters on this journey, for showing me the ways that you love your bodies. For showing me the ways that you don't.

To my parents, for giving me life, for fusing your chromosomes to create this body of mine, for always doing your best to love and care for me.

To my friends and family, for loving and encouraging me and promising to read this book. You are too many to name individually, but I love each and every one of you.

To the person who donated their body so I could receive their cadaver bone and heal from a terrible accident with less pain. Along with Mary Roach and her book *Stiff,* you've inspired me to donate my body when I die.

To my teachers, whose activism and leadership have taught me how to embrace myself, specifically Sonya Renee Taylor, author of *The Body Is Not an Apology*, Taryn Brumfit and the Body Image Movement, and especially, Elizabeth Dialto, Wild Soul Movement maven. Your influence has ripples.

To my Marni, for asking the hard questions and guiding me on the healing path to fully loving myself. Love U!

To my editor, Tanya Gold, for your brilliant and incisive suggestions and for the praise that always arrived just when I needed it most.

To my beta readers, for your insightful comments and the encouragement that let me know I was on the right path.

To my proofreader, Crystal Watanabe, for your keen eye, careful reading, and kind words.

To my photographers, Cass Bradley and Corrie Fewell, for capturing my power and the beauty of my family in breathtaking photos.

To my fabulous team at SPARK Publications, for understanding my vision, for providing unwavering support, and for helping me share this empowering message with women.

To my Mica, for being my partner, for creating the images that make my words leap off the page. I love them, and I love you.

To my daughters, Campbell Faye and Jude Rae, for being mirrors, for showing me how worthy I am of wide and deep self-love. I hope you always love yourselves and your bodies fiercely, because you are wonderfully made.

To my husband, Terry, who has always loved my body, especially when I couldn't. I love you so, so much. You're my favorite, my touchstone (insert bawdy joke here), my partner in life—thank you for everything.

Photo courtesy of Corrie Fewell, BlueSky Photo Artists

Photo courtesy of Cass Bradley, Find My Fearless

About the Author

Nicole C. Ayers has been playing with words as long as she can remember. While she's held many jobs in her life, including stints as a server, camp counselor, telemarketer, print-shop lackey, bartender, and teacher, editing at Ayers Edits was her favorite, because she combined her love of reading with the fun of wordplay, until she added writer to this list. Now it would be hard to convince her there's anything better than telling her own stories.

Nicole is the author of *Love Notes to My Body; Love Letters to My Body: Writing My Way to (Self-)Love;* and *Writing Your Way to (Self-)Love: A Guided Journal to Help You Love Your Body, One Part at a Time.*

Nicole lives in South Carolina with her brilliant and brave daughters, her best friend and husband, a goofy dog, a long-suffering tortoise, and the occasional fish.

Contact Nicole at NicoleCAyers.com and connect with her on Instagram at @nicolecayers.

An Invitation

Thank you so much for reading *Love Letters to My Body*. If you're compelled to explore your own relationship with your body, please check out *Writing Your Way to (Self-) Love: A Guided Journal to Help You Love Your Body, One Part at a Time*, where I walk you through my own practice with love and encouragement so that you, too, can give it a whirl.

And if you enjoyed these essays, you may also enjoy *Love Notes to My Body*, a beautifully illustrated book that brought me so much joy to create with my dear friend and illustrator, Mica Gadhia. It's lighthearted and fun and whimsical.

Please leave a review on Amazon or Goodreads or wherever you purchased the book so that others can find it, too.

Visit my website—NicoleCAyers.com—and sign up for my newsletter, Love Notes, for first looks at new essays, spotlights on people to follow, book recommendations, and more. You can join me on Instagram, too: @nicolecayers.

Love, Nicole

www.ingramcontent.com/pod-product-compliance
Lightning Source LLC
Chambersburg PA
CBHW050330120526
44592CB00014B/2121